A Voice for Rose

by Anna Pianfetti Eccher

Bless the beasts and the children
For in this world they have no voice
They have no choice

Bless the beasts and the children
For the world can never be
The world they see

The Carpenters

Acknowledgements

For all those who helped me on my journey of knowing my Aunt Rose and bringing her home, I thank you. You know who you are. Without your help, none of this would have been possible. If I have omitted anyone, please forgive me. My heartfelt thanks:

- To my husband Greg, for allowing me to be me. Always.
- To my children Maggie, Patsy, and Dominic and grandchildren, Davey, Tillie, and any more grandchildren we may be blessed with. These truths are for you. Always remember who you came from.
- To my mom and dad, for always believing in me.
- To Joan, my cousin by blood and my sister in spirit, whom I found because of Rose. My life has been made richer because we are family.
- To Vicky, for helping us bring Rose's ashes home.
- To Richard Stilwell, for early encouragement and editing.
- To Ed Becker, for all your help bringing Rose home and giving her a homecoming.
- To Mike Mathis, for your encouragement and assistance with the records.
- To the funeral home where Rose was initially buried and their staff. Thank you for helping Rose find her way back home.
- To the members of the Carlinville Writers Guild and especially the Tuesday write-in group. You kept me going.
- Lastly, to Rose and all my family whose words were forever frozen in the records. Thank you for your guidance and strength. You are with me always.

Author's Forward

I would never have dreamed that this journey Aunt Rose and I have shared would have ever been possible. Being able to obtain her records allowed me to read and begin to understand how my family arrived at the decisions they made. However, it didn't take long to realize that in order to truly understand Rose's story, I would also need to know Rose's mother's (my grandmother's) story. Both these women were victims of the time they lived in, and their stories were intertwined. Learning about their lives also shed light on my father's life as well.

Along the way, I had some people tell me that looking into my aunt's past might not be a good idea. Finding her records might reveal things I didn't want to know – painful, hurtful things. My answer to that has always been that the truth can set you free. I always hoped that it would set Rose free. Her truths needed to be known, for her and for my family. What I also learned along this journey is that many families have secrets and family stories stuffed way down deep. We are all human; we all hurt; but we can heal.

As much as this story is for Rose – her way of finally being able to have a voice and have her truths known – it is also for all the other Roses that have been, are now, or ever might be, and for all their families. Shame and guilt can be powerful forces, and it's my deep desire that Rose's story will help others with similar stories to no longer feel or carry any shame or guilt. This is my hope and my prayer.

Anna

The author can be reached at annapianfettieccher@gmail.com.

Part I: Rose's Story

Part II: Finding Rose; Bringing Her Home

Part I: Rose's Story

My name is Rose. I was only seventeen years old when I was committed to Alton State Mental Hospital in 1953. I begged not to be left there because I knew no one in my family would come back for me. Like so many others of my generation, I was committed to a state mental institution simply because no one understood how to help me. The long days turned into weeks, months, and then years. Five long decades of incarceration would be my sentence. I had to believe that one day, no matter how long it might take, my exile would end. When God knew the time was right, I would be found. Then, in 2009, after 56 long years, someone finally came for me. My niece found me and brought me home to be buried next to my mother and grandmother. After so many lost years, I am at rest. I am home. This is my story.

Chapter 1

A Difficult Birth

My journey into this world began on June 10, 1935. I wouldn't enter this world easily. Mine wasn't an easy delivery for my mother, Helen.

My parents had married just a year before my birth. My mother came from a strict German family, while my father, Mario, was the only child of Italian immigrants. Their union was not looked upon favorably by my mother's family. My mother's parents didn't approve of what my father did for a living. He would loosely describe himself as a "general laborer," but everyone knew his occupation was questionable.

The small town of Benld, Illinois, where I was born, was known to be a bit of a rough-and-tumble place. Gambling, prostitution, and drinking thrived in this small town. Benld was known to have more taverns than churches. Rumor had it that Al Capone himself would visit Benld when "the heat was on in Chicago," a rumor never proven but widely believed. There were many illegal activities to be found by a good-looking Italian man in 1930's Benld, and my father never seemed to have any trouble finding them.

It could easily be said that my mother found her future husband to be charming and attractive. His easy Italian manner, natural good looks, and steady flow of ready cash made him irresistible to the shy German girl with strict parents. His red convertible didn't hurt matters, either. Was it love or lust? No one will ever know except for them. Their union would produce two children – me and my brother Dominic.

My parents named me after my father's mother, Rosa. Since my father was an only child, my impending birth was an event met with great pride and anticipation by him and his Italian immigrant family. I would be an only daughter and the only granddaughter for my father's parents. You might think this would be enough to keep me safe in the years to come, but it wasn't.

My mother's labor was excruciatingly long, lasting for hours, and it would end with a birth that was more frightening than the labor itself. In 1935, babies were born at home, where many things could and often did go wrong. Many mothers and babies died from complications. We were lucky enough to have a physician at my birth. Because of this, my mother and I would both survive. Some would say our survival was a blessing; others would think the opposite.

I was born feet first. Breech is the term that is used today. During a breech delivery in 1935, with the limited knowledge of the times and a home delivery the only alternative, all anyone could really do was hope for the best. I began my journey into this world by being pulled feet first from my mother's womb. I was pulled so hard and with such force, a tendon in my neck was stretched. My head would permanently tilt to the left until I reached the age of seven and a half, when I would undergo surgery in an attempt to straighten my head. This surgery would leave me with a deep scar that would always make me feel self-conscious and ugly, a forever reminder of my fight to enter this world.

I have wondered many times what exactly happened in that room, shortly after midnight, as I entered this world, pulled and yanked into the dark, early morning. My mother, who was surely beyond exhaustion, must have been overwhelmed by the horror of my birth, which she had expected to go smoothly. My father must have felt sheer terror at the thought of losing both his wife and his new daughter. I can only think there must have been fear in the doctor's eyes, knowing that most births such as these rarely ended well for mother or child.

I can imagine my mother asking, fear creeping into her cracked voice, "Is it a girl? Is she all right?" I'm sure she knew, by the hesitation in the doctor's voice, that I was not all right. "Yes, it's a girl, Helen," the doctor answered. His omission of whether I was all right gave my mother the answer she feared.

I know I was deprived of oxygen during my birth as I was ripped from my mother, the tendons in my neck rupturing and tearing. There was also a lack of blood flow through my umbilical cord, causing me to suffer fetal brain damage. I experienced damage to my eyes as my head was being pulled from my mother's pelvis. My eyes needed treatment shortly after my birth; hence the poor eyesight that plagued me all my life. My internal organs were damaged during my delivery and would later cause me to experience enuresis, an uncontrollable discharge of urine, for most of my life.

It's hard to say whether any of these things on their own were the cause of my impending doom. But when all of these pieces are put together – my injured head, the brain damage, the poor eyesight, and the enuresis – it is easy to see that my fragile beginning would most certainly set the stage for the unkind hand that fate would later deal me.

There are many questions about my birth that will never be fully answered. The long labor and delivery, the mental and physical toll the birth took on my mother, my physical imperfections – did all these things cause my mother not to want me or know how to take care of me? Is that why at the age of 18 months I would be sent to live with her parents, my grandparents?

I do know that my mother wrestled with her own demons all her life, and I think caring for me was something she just wasn't capable of doing. Perhaps the effects of my birth were beginning to be seen, and it was becoming obvious that my development wasn't progressing normally compared to other children my age. The birth of my younger brother fifteen months later would go smoothly, and it would quickly become apparent that his development was normal. Perhaps it was then that I was beginning to be seen, as I would be for the rest of my life, as a burden.

No one considered the effects a breech birth might have had on me. In the 1940's and 1950's, phrases such as "developmentally disabled" were neither used nor understood. I might have had a form of autism, but that condition had not yet been identified by the medical profession. I was born in the wrong generation, to people who didn't know how to help me. My family committed me to Alton State Hospital when I was 17 years old in 1953. For over half a century, I would be moved to so many different state institutions that even I lost track. But what I do know is that from the day I was committed in 1953, I would never see any of my family ever again. I was banished, my only crime being that no one understood or knew what to do with me. During my long years of institutionalization, the only thing I dreamed of, the only thing I held onto, was the hope that one day, somehow, I would get to go home again.

Chapter 2

My Early Years

When I was just 18 months old in 1937, I went to live in my grandparents' home in Mt. Olive, Illinois. Except for a couple of years when I lived with my mother, this was the house that I would grow up in, living with my grandparents and my uncle, until my incarceration at age 17. With all my problems, everyone felt it would be best for me to live there since my mother and stepfather's home was not stable.

I lived with my mother from age six to age eight, with six of those months spent in a sanitarium in Springfield, Illinois, where I received surgery to repair the torticollis that resulted from my difficult birth.

My neck was twisted, and my head tipped to one side while my chin turned to the other. I arrived at the sanitarium on June 15, 1943, where I remained until October 31, 1943. (See photo on next page.) It would take four-and-a-half months and two painful surgeries to finally allow me to hold my head straight for the first time in my life. The surgery corrected my pulled tendon which had stretched my head to the left. The surgeries would entail the division of my sternocleidomastoid

St. John's Sanitarium in Springfield, Illinois, where Rose had corrective surgery on her neck in 1943.

muscle to my sternum and clavicle. They had to completely divide my sternocleidomastoid muscle, and I had to wear a body cast from my neck to my waist for six months. These surgeries would leave me with the scar that I hated and tried for so many years to hide.

Although I was initially scared to go there, my time at the sanitarium was good. The people there, especially the Sisters of St. Francis, were very kind to me. Even though the surgery was difficult, I loved all the people there. The Hospital Sisters of St. Francis became like mothers to me. They spoiled me and made sure I was well taken care of. I had to wear my cast for a long time, and I think the sisters worried about how I would get along when I went home. Part of me never wanted to leave there, but I knew I couldn't stay. The other children and I would play tag in the hallways, laughing and running until one of the sisters would tell us to stop. The other children that were there also had something wrong with them, and we accepted each other because we knew what it felt like to be different. The surgery was successful, and my head would finally look somewhat normal, but I fell behind in my schoolwork during this time. I had to repeat the first grade and later, the fifth grade as well.

After my surgery, I went back home to live with my mother for a few months more until returning to my grandparents' house to live. Things were not good at my mother's house, and I would never go back to live with her again. My grandmother was good to me, even though she was older and caring for me couldn't have been easy for her. For the most part, I got along well with my grandparents, though they were very strict. Raising a young child, especially one with special needs, after they had already raised their own three children, was probably not a job they had expected to do.

My grandfather knew that I struggled and had to try harder to do things than other children. On the rare occasion when a friend would come over to play, he would make them apologize to me if they made fun of me. When my grandfather died in 1951, I lost the one person who had ever tried to be an advocate for me. He was the only father figure I would ever know, since my own father had died when I was just six years old.

Unfortunately, my grandfather could not be with me all the time, and there was no one else to stand up for me when my classmates would make fun of me and call me names. It took me a long time to learn new things, and I had to go over them many times in order to understand. When I attended grade school, I was called names, and no one in the class wanted to sit next to me because they said I smelled. What they didn't know or understand is that the injury to my bladder, caused by my traumatic birth, left me unable to control my urine flow. What many viewed as my failure to keep myself clean was really a medical problem that no one helped me deal with. No matter how hard I tried, I was always suffering another accident. My own family found it difficult to help me. I was accused of not trying hard enough to make sure I went to the bathroom when I needed to. No one ever seemed to consider that perhaps my problem was out of my control. No matter how hard I tried, I would inevitably have another accident. I got used to being made fun of. It just became the way it was.

The only time I felt safe from the teasing and ridicule was when I was at my grandparents' house. Their house became my sanctuary, my refuge from the sadness that followed me throughout my childhood years. I spent so much time inside this house that many people in the town I grew up in didn't even know I existed. It was as if I became part of the house, almost as if the house "took me in." It was the only home I would ever know, and Mt. Olive would be the only place I would ever call home. I would spend most of my life trying to find my way back there.

Mt. Olive was a small town that was home to a multitude of ethnic populations. Many of the people who lived there had come to the town in the early 1900's to be reunited with family members who had previously immigrated. The idea of being surrounded by people who shared their beliefs and the opportunities for work were the main reasons most people settled in our town. My grandfather had immigrated from Germany with his large, proud German Lutheran family. Five of the twelve children in his family came from my great-grandfather's first wife and the other seven from his second wife after his first wife died. Mt. Olive was a good place for his family to settle, as many other Germans had also made their homes there.

Main Street was the hub of the town, where everything a person needed could be found at one of its small, family-owned shops. Most of the men were coal miners since mining was the main source of jobs in the area. Everyone knew one another in Mt. Olive. All you needed to do was say your name and everyone knew who you were or who you were related to. A family's name and reputation were extremely important. I think this is one of the reasons I always felt so inadequate around other people. I tried so hard to be the normal girl I knew my family wished I could be. I know they made excuses for me and my behavior. It was hard to explain me to other people, and I know even my family found it hard to tolerate me and how different I was.

As I was growing up, the kitchen was my favorite room in the house. This was the one room where I always felt I belonged. It was in this room that I would help cook meals, set the table, and wash the dishes. The kitchen made me feel important. It was where I felt like I could actually do something, that I could feel part of something. Working in the kitchen was one of the few times I could feel good about myself because I could do things my way. My grandmother could never understand why I would insist on resetting the table after she had already set it. I would take all the dishes off the table and then reset the table my way. I needed everything on the table to be placed in a certain position. My grandmother would just shake her head and mutter, "Rose, Rose, why are you always redoing what I've already done?" I couldn't explain it to her. I just knew I needed it to be done a certain way, my way.

The one piece of furniture in the kitchen that my grandmother treasured was a white cupboard. One of my best memories of her is of watching her sit at that cupboard writing letters. I always felt so safe when I could look over and see her sitting there, her hand swiftly moving back and forth over the writing paper, sharing her life with her sisters through her letters. It would be these memories from this kitchen, from this house, that would sustain me in the years ahead. These memories needed to be strong and clear, for they would be all I would have to hold onto in the years ahead.

There was another room in the house that was just as important to me as the kitchen – my bedroom in the attic, where I spent nearly all my time. In order to get up to the attic, you had to climb an old, narrow, wooden flight of stairs that were mostly hidden in the corner of the room. I loved spending time upstairs because this was where I could pretend, where I could play without fear of ridicule. Also, some of my mother's things were stored in the attic, and since her things were as close to her as I could get, I treasured every minute I spent there. I would hear my grandfather calling from downstairs,

"Rose, come down here for a while. You've been up there all day!" I would never answer, as I was too busy to be bothered. I was busy talking to my mother, asking her why she wasn't here and why she always seemed so sad when I did see her. Even though she was not there to answer me, I would keep asking her questions, always hoping she would somehow hear me. One thing never changed – no matter how many times I sat in the attic and asked questions of my invisible mother, I would never get any answers.

Years in the future, the attic would prove to be very important for me. It would become my memory keeper where I left my possessions so that one day someone might find them and know that I had existed. It would keep my few possessions safe for over half a century.

Chapter 3

My Mother Goes Away

Even though I didn't live with her, my heart was broken when my stepfather had my mother committed to a state hospital when I was only 13 years old. Every day after she left, I longed and cried for her. It did no good; she was gone. Before she left, I'd go and visit her almost every day, even though I didn't live with her. I didn't know it at the time, but I would never see my mother again once she was committed. At the age of 13, I really needed her, but she was gone and would never be able to help me again, especially after I myself would be sent away. There would be no one to help me then.

Everyone said that my mother was crazy. What I remember most about her is that she cried a lot. I also remember that my stepfather was mean to her. She was a nervous woman, and it was easy for my stepfather to have her committed to Alton State Hospital in 1949. Because of this, it would prove to be even easier, four years later, to say that I, too, was crazy and should be sent away, just like my mother. What no one understood at the time was that she needed help. She needed to get as far away from her abusive second husband as she could. She suffered from manic depression, which is now called bipolar. In 1949, this illness wasn't understood the way it is today. Mental illness was not something talked about and, without the right treatment, my mother just slipped further and further into herself.

My mother had never finished high school. Her second husband made all the decisions in their home and provided what little money they had. His best friend was alcohol; therefore, he never knew what a steady job was, so he was able to focus much of his energy on ridiculing and shaming his wife. He became very good at it.

My mother depended on her second husband for everything. She had failed in her first marriage, having divorced my father when I was only four years old. This was a shameful thing for my family. Her new husband thought she should feel lucky that he had married a divorced woman. He felt she should be grateful to have him. She easily became his victim.

"Why is he mean to you?" I would ask my mother.

"Oh, Rose, he doesn't mean to be," she'd always say. "I just need to be better, stop crying, and be quiet so he can rest. My crying makes him upset. Don't worry, I'll be fine."

But I did worry for her. "He's mean and makes you cry, and then I cry," I would tell my mother.

My mother would smile nervously, her eyes darting about, as if she was looking for something she knew she could never find. She would confide in some of her close neighbors, but all they could do was offer a sympathetic ear. No one knew how to help her, and no one really wanted to get involved. Sometimes when the abuse got really bad, my grandmother would go to my mother's house to try to "straighten things out," but it never seemed to help.

Then one day when I walked to her house to visit her, she was gone. Just like that. Gone. I knew then that what little I'd known of my mother was no more and never would be again.

My stepfather was sitting on the back porch. "She's gone, Rose. I had to send her away." That was my stepfather's answer when I asked him where she was.

"Why?" I asked. "Why did you send her away?"

"Doctor says she needs treatment," he said. "Always sitting around here crying for no reason. Always acting sad and scared." I could tell he was beginning to get mad, and I knew what would happen once he did.

"Doctor says she needs the shock therapy, you know, those electric shock treatments they give them in the crazy house. That's where I sent her."

I didn't know what electric shock therapy was, but one day soon, that would change.

"And you know, Rose, you'd better be careful," he said in a menacing tone, his voice scaring me now more than ever, "or you'll end up as crazy as your mother, and we might have to send you away!"

I ran from that house that day, faster than I had ever run before in my life, and I never went back. I ran not just from the house, but from the words, the words that kept filling my head even as I was running. Those words would follow me, and I'd hear those words time and time again, from many other people. What I didn't know then was that words, when said by enough people, sometimes have the power of making things come true.

I didn't understand where they had sent my mother, and I cried for her for what seemed like forever. Many people would say that she hadn't been a good mother, and I do know that she never really loved me the same way she loved my brother, since I was physically flawed and considered "slow." I think she somehow blamed herself for my birth imperfections. She saw her failure in me every time she looked at me. But she was my mother, and no matter how she saw me, I never gave up hope, all through the long years ahead, that one day, somehow, we would be together again.

Once she was gone, I seemed to drift aimlessly. The ridicule I suffered from my classmates got worse after my mother was sent away, and it was becoming harder for me to keep up with my schoolwork. I was able to do all right with my reading assignments, and I loved the history lessons, but math proved to be a formidable opponent. Even though I liked my teachers, I began to fall so far behind in my lessons that it soon became clear that I would never be able to catch up. It was just as well because it had become unbearable for me to listen to the constant taunts that had become a part of my daily life.

"Did you hear about Rose's mother? She went crazy, and they had to send her away," they would whisper. "Poor Rose is as crazy as her mother."

I only wanted to have friends and be accepted, but that was impossible now. Even my own brother began to distance himself from me. He didn't want to be ridiculed the way I was, and it became easy for him to just ignore me. I know it was hard for him, too, but he gave up on me, just like everyone else did. We were motherless children now, he and I, and the world is not kind to motherless children. My brother entered survival mode, and the only one he could save was himself. Years later, he would pay for this decision. His guilt would eat at him, and a sadness would follow him forever, a sadness he would try to drink away. But the alcohol never wiped me from his memory; I was always there. If I could've said one thing to my brother, I would've told him that I understood. I would've told him that I

forgave him and loved him, no matter what he had said to me,

and that I knew he wouldn't have been able to save me. My

brother and I came from the same people and the same place,

and all I ever wanted was for him to accept me for who I was.

He had no one to help him do that. I know how hard it was for

us, orphans that we were, trying to survive and fit in when

everyone around us believed our mother was crazy.

My brother didn't have it any easier than I did once our

mother was sent away. He stayed with my stepfather and

almost starved to death. Making sure a young boy had food to

eat was not a priority in my stepfather's house. My brother was

left to fend for himself, and the day after he graduated high

school, he joined the Marines, getting as far away from it as fast

as he possibly could.

Chapter 4

Life After My Mother

After my mother was gone, I did at least finish the eighth grade. I attempted high school, but the teasing had gotten worse. At least when I was at my grandparents' house, I had a routine, one that made me feel safe. I think if the Bad Thing hadn't happened, I could have remained forever at my grandparents' house and been happy there. The Bad Thing changed all that. I don't like to talk about the Bad Thing because sometimes people made me feel like it was my fault that it happened, that maybe I could've done something to stop it.

I did try to go to high school, but it wasn't just the schoolwork that made me feel bad about myself. Some teachers tried to help me, but it never seemed to work out. Once, I attended a dance at the school, and one of my teachers asked the boys if any of them would please dance with me. I was so sure one of them would. I had spent a lot of time getting ready for the dance and had worked a long time on my hair. My hair was unruly and had a mind of its own. No matter how much I tried to brush it or pin it down, it would always come undone

Rose sitting on the front porch of her grandparents' house in Mt. Olive, Illinois.

and look wild and unkempt. The day of the dance, though, I thought it looked nice, as nice as I could get it to look. I had brushed it enough so that it lay as flat as it could around my face. Surely with my hair looking so pretty, someone would ask me to dance. (See above photo.) But no one did. I'm not sure which was worse – no one asking me to dance, or the shame I felt just standing there with everyone looking at me, whispering about me.

"Poor Rose," I knew they were thinking, "she can't even get one boy to dance with her."

I never went to another dance after that, and it wouldn't be much longer before I would totally drop out of school forever. I started to retreat into myself more and more after this, and I think that's why my family decided it would be best to send me away. Although I didn't go to church very often, my grandparents were strict German Lutherans. They would've never wanted me to attend Catholic services, so I'm not sure who made the decision to send me to St. John's Sanitarium in Springfield, Illinois, in 1952. Maybe it was because this is where I had stayed for six months several years earlier when I'd had the surgery to correct my neck.

I not only worked at the sanitarium but also tried to attend classes in the school there. I think sending me to Springfield was my family's way of being able to say that they had done everything within their power to help me. I failed miserably there. I was expected to work during the week, as well as do my schoolwork. I made nineteen dollars per week and also earned my room and board. The girls were nice to me, much nicer than back home, but I was too busy to have a chance to become friends with them. It only took two weeks for me to fall behind in my schoolwork. The math was impossible for me to understand, just as it had been back home. I could only stay in school for two weeks because I was unable to get both my schoolwork done and carry out my work duties.

I needed a strict schedule and didn't do well when I felt overwhelmed, as I did the entire time I was at St. John's. It made me very nervous when things didn't go smoothly. I felt as if everything was slipping out from under me, like I was drowning and couldn't get any air. I don't even remember why, but one day I wandered away. I wanted to go home, back to the safety of my grandparents' house. I didn't know how to get there. I walked for what seemed like a long time, and all the streets looked the same. I was lost.

39

"Rose, here," I heard a voice calling to me. The voice sounded like it was coming through a thick, heavy veil of fog, but sounded somehow familiar. "Rose, come here, over here." Now I recognized the voice as my uncle's. He had come for me. As much as I wanted to go back home, I knew that if I went with him, I'd not stay long and would be sent away again. But I had no choice. I had no mother or father to come for me, so I had to go with him. Somehow, deep inside, I knew this was the beginning of the end for me.

Chapter 5

The Beginning of the End

Once I was back in Mt. Olive, I tried hard to fit in, but the things I did never seemed to be right or good enough, unlike my brother, who always seemed to do the right thing. I was jealous of him because things just seemed to be so easy for him. At least, that's what I thought. What I didn't know was that after our mother was sent away, things were anything but easy for him. While living at our mother's house with our stepfather, my brother was hungry most of the time. He began what would become his normal routine, scurrying from house to house to find a meal. He relied on the kindness of others, never complaining since he knew it wouldn't help anyway. I'm not sure why my brother stayed with our stepfather and didn't come to live with our grandparents. Perhaps living with me was just too hard for him.

My family said I started to get worse after I returned from the sanitarium. I seemed to be more nervous and had started talking to myself. They thought it seemed as if I was hearing voices. They noticed that I had lost interest in television and didn't care if company came over or not. I kept to myself, but I loved to listen to the radio. I spent most of my time in my bedroom, up in the attic. I used to go up and lie down immediately after eating. I had to be very careful about what I ate because I became convinced there was poison in the canned food, and I refused to eat anything that came from a can. I don't know why it was so hard for my family to understand why I couldn't eat this food, but I really believed it would make me sick.

I had always spent most of my time up in the attic, and I started to spend more and more time there after returning from Springfield. I think that's why most people in town never really knew much about me. Those who knew my brother never even knew I existed. It was almost as if I was a ghost. Rose the ghost.

When I did try to go out and do errands, it never seemed to go well. I would go to the local grocery store to get food, but it would take me a long time to get what I needed, and the store clerks didn't like me being in there very long. Sometimes it felt as if people were watching me and talking about me. People didn't understand that I just needed to take my time so I could get exactly what I needed and make sure everything was in order. I needed things to be neat and orderly and not out of sequence. It was the same way with my lists. In my notebook, I would write long lists of the items I bought in the store, and I didn't want anyone looking at them. They were MY lists. It made me nervous if anyone paged through my notebook and touched the pages.

I liked to help my grandmother with the chores, but I needed it to be done my way. No one ever understood that. If there were rugs outside that needed to be shaken, I would shake them over and over until I knew there was no dirt left on them. This seemed to make everyone nervous.

"Rose," they'd say, "stop it. The rugs are clean. Come in the house now." But I knew I had to keep going until I was done, no matter how long it took. I think I embarrassed them.

When I ran the sweeper in the house, I would run it much longer than anyone else would. I could never get them to understand that I needed the house to be clean and needed to do it my way, even if it meant doing it over and over. Why couldn't they see that I just wanted it done right? Sometimes it made my head hurt, making sure everything was done the way I needed it to be.

After the eighth grade, once my mother was sent away, I didn't have many friends. Most of the girls just wanted to make fun of me once they knew she was gone. When I was younger and did have friends, I seemed to be "stuck to them," as my grandmother would say. I was very shy around strangers, and it was hard for me to make friends, though I was always friendly with people that I already knew. That's what scared me so much about the Bad Thing. I always thought that people you knew wouldn't hurt you, but I was wrong. After the Bad Thing, I never really trusted anyone ever again. But I don't want to talk about that now.

One friend I had, Erma, would walk with me to school in the morning. When we were in the second grade, Erma was taller and lankier than I. I craved attention, and having a friend helped me feel like I somehow fit in with other people. Unfortunately, that feeling would never last for too long.

I went everywhere with Erma, and often when we walked to school, we would stop at this one house. The nice lady who lived there would serve us toast and hot tea for breakfast. I think she knew that Erma and I needed a little extra help, and she was kind enough to share her family's food with us. Even though we never told her, I hope she knew just how much her acts of kindness meant to Erma and me.

Rose standing beside her grandparent's house in Mt. Olive, Illinois.

I remember my grandmother used to always tell me that I was kind. I knew this must be a good thing because of the way she would say it, like she was finally proud of me for doing something right. My brother was usually the only one receiving praise, since he was smarter than me. Sometimes I was able to do things for other people, and it always made me feel good. (See above photo.) For a few months, I helped an older woman who lived in our neighborhood with her housework. I was a good worker, and my neighbor seemed to appreciate that I liked things to be neat and in their place. She was always very kind to me. But just like everything else I ever did in my life, I wouldn't be able to do this for very long, either.

Chapter 6

St. Vincent's

In early 1953, when I was just 17 years old, my family felt they could no longer keep me at home because of the way I was acting. My appetite was poor, and I had a hard time swallowing the food everyone wanted me to eat. I was much less active than I had been, and I didn't want to talk much. It was difficult for me to concentrate. I would sometimes just stare off into space. At other times, I would be looking for something I just wasn't able to find, and I couldn't even explain to anyone what I was searching for.

I didn't care how I looked or what I wore, and I was always being told to "get myself together," but I never could do that. That's why, in March 1953, I was sent to St. Vincent's Hospital. It was a Catholic hospital in Normandy, Missouri, that was operated by the Sisters of Charity of Vincent de Saint Paul. (See photo on next page.) The hospital specialized in the treatment of nervous and mental disorders, including cases of drug addiction and alcoholism. Patient fees helped to finance the hospital, and there was no way I could have been sent there unless my family had the means to finance my stay.

St. Vincent's Hospital in Normandy, Missouri.

My family wasn't wealthy and couldn't have afforded for me to go there. Although my father was dead, my paternal grandfather had set up a trust fund for me and my brother. The proceeds of this trust paid for me to go to St. Vincent's. However, the money ran out after just six weeks. I had to be discharged even though the doctors at St. Vincent's said that I needed more treatment.

It was during my stay at St. Vincent's that I first heard the words Electroconvulsive Therapy (ECT). I was given eight ECT treatments during my six-week stay at St. Vincent's. I now knew what it was like to receive the shock therapy that my mother had suffered when she was sent away. We finally had something in common, my mother and I. Except for the Bad Thing, shock therapy was the worst thing that had ever happened to me.

Nothing could have ever prepared me for receiving these treatments. I was only 17 years old, and all I knew was that I was going to be given the same thing my mother had been given years ago when she was sent away. All I had ever been told was that shock therapy was for crazy people, so that must have meant I was crazy, too. The day I received my first treatment, I had no idea what would happen.

Two nice nurses came into my room and asked if I wanted to take a walk.

"Yes," I said. "Where are we going?" I was hoping that maybe I was going home. I was sure my family missed me and wanted me to come home.

"Oh, don't you worry about where we're going, you're going to be fine now, just fine," said one of the nice nurses. I wasn't quite sure what it was about the tone of the nurse's voice when she answered me, but somehow I knew, deep down in my insides, that I was not going to be fine.

I had no choice but to go with them, especially since each nurse had a grip on one of my arms and was leading me out of the room and down the hallway. I couldn't walk very fast and shuffled down the hallway. I made loud noises as I walked, and I wondered if anyone would hear and try to stop us.

"What is all that noise in the hallway?" someone might ask. But no one said anything, so we kept on walking, I and the nice nurses.

At the end of the hallway, we came to a room with the door closed. Chairs were lined up on either side of the door. One of the nurses told me I couldn't go in the room just yet, that I had to wait my turn.

"Now, just sit here a spell, Rose, it won't be very long." *How nice,* I thought, *I will wait my turn, just like I used to do at school.* I was good at waiting my turn. I sat nicely in the chair, trying to remember what it was like to be in school, when I heard the first scream. The blood froze in my veins. My head jerked straight up, and I turned towards the door, as if looking at the door could somehow make the screaming stop. I thought someone was dying in there, and I was next. I would die next. I must have started shaking, because one of the nurses brought a blanket and put it around my shoulders.

"There you go, Rose, that should warm you up a bit." *I'm not cold,* I wanted to tell her, *I'm scared. I'm scared I'm going to die. I don't want to go into that room.* I couldn't get the words to come out of my mouth, so I just looked up at her with tears streaming down my face.

And then, somehow, I knew it was my turn. I think it was the way the two nice nurses were coming towards me. I knew they were coming to help me out of my chair, and I knew this was the end for me. They took the blanket off my shoulders and helped to steady me as I got up on my feet. Slowly, we made our way into the room. I tried to pull away from the two nice nurses, but I couldn't get my body to move out of their grip. They were so strong. I knew right then that they were not nice, like I had thought. They were mean, and I knew that wherever they were taking me would not be a good place.

"I don't want to go in there," I heard myself saying to the nurses.

"Oh, Rose, come on now, it won't be so bad. We're here to help you. You'll feel so much better after you're done," one of them said.

"That's right, Rose, you'll feel all better once you're done and then you can rest," the other nurse said. For just a second, I thought that maybe I should try to be good and just go with them and not complain.

I knew my mother had endured this, so a part of me thought that maybe I should stop fighting and go in the room with the nurses. Still, something deep inside me just didn't feel right. I knew that this wouldn't be a good thing, and I couldn't stop my fear from choking my words as they came out of my mouth.

"Please, please don't make me go in there. Please let me go. I won't be any trouble, I promise."

No amount of pleading would help me. This therapy was what the doctor had ordered, so this is what I'd have to do. I'd learned long ago that what I wanted was not important, and this was just more proof of how little control I had over my life. Maybe the doctor and the nurses were right, maybe this treatment would help me. All I knew was that my mother had gotten the same treatment when they sent her away. She hadn't come home. It hadn't helped her.

So, into the room I went, led by the women dressed in white, one on either side of me, pulling me helplessly into a room that I was sure I would never come out of. There was a doctor in the room and another man dressed in white. It was as if they had been waiting just for me.

"Please bring her over here and help her lie down on the table," I heard the doctor say. "That's it, Rose, just come on over here. Everything will be just fine." As I was being pulled over to the table, I briefly wondered if my mother had heard the same words before she had received her therapy.

It was as if I was outside myself, almost as if I was someone else, watching the nurses half drag me up onto the table. I couldn't move my arms or legs, and my lips quivered when my body touched the ice-cold, stainless-steel table. The nurses

54

made me lie down, and I remember one of them saying something to me, though I couldn't quite make out what it was. I felt like I was in a fog and everyone's mouths were moving slower than the sounds they were making. It was as if everything was in slow motion. When I looked down, I could see that my hands were tied down, one on each side of me. I tried to lift one of them but couldn't. *That is odd,* I thought. *Why can't I move my hand?* I felt someone, maybe a nurse, patting my arm, her mouth moving slowly, saying something that sounded like, "Don't worry, Rose, this will all be over soon enough."

Then I felt something cold on each side of my head, so cold that my head jerked upwards, and I could feel someone's hands trying to steady my head on the table.

"Hold your head still, Rose," I heard someone saying. *Why did they need me to hold my head still?* I wondered. It felt so cold. I wondered what they were putting on me as my brain tried to take in what was happening. They were trying to put something on my head, and I was fighting them as hard as I could. It felt cold and tight on my head. Something was being held in my mouth, and I wasn't sure what is was. Someone was holding my mouth closed and lifting my chin up. It hurt, but I couldn't say anything. I could hear people talking. I felt a jolt. That's the last thing I remembered until I woke up in my bed.

Even though I knew I still needed help, I didn't want any more shock treatments. I was hoping there was some other way to help me. Since the money had run out, there was nothing left to do but send me home. As happy as I was to be going home, something deep inside me made me feel the worst was yet to come.

Chapter 7

Sent Away

When I returned from St. Vincent's, I stayed at my grandmother's house for what seemed like a long time. I hardly ever left the house. I was so tired, and my head hurt. It felt good just to sleep, and I was so glad to be home. I spent nearly all my time in my bedroom, just sleeping. I felt sleepy all the time.

I could hear my grandmother yelling, "Rose, why don't you come to the table and get something to eat?" But by now, I wasn't even going to the kitchen to eat.

"I can't come," I'd try to shout back. "I'm too tired. I just want to sleep." Usually my grandmother would end up bringing me a tray with some food on it.

Even though she was glad I was home, it was hard for my grandmother to take care of me. I wondered why I just couldn't seem to get up and eat or try to get up to help her with things. It all just seemed so impossible for me to do anything.

But one day, and I don't really know why, I decided to get up and take a walk. I hadn't been out in weeks, so I know I must've looked a sight with my rumpled dress and my wild hair tumbling all over my head. My family didn't want me to leave the house. I walked up and down the street aimlessly and eventually wound up at the local newspaper office. I decided that the office needed to be cleaned because of all the dirty, untrue things they were printing. I started cleaning and kept cleaning even when the staff asked me to stop.

They called the police. This would prove to be the last thing my family could tolerate. I'm sure they were tired of me embarrassing them. They called the local doctor, who quickly told my family that they would need to send me away again, but this time I wouldn't be coming home any time soon. If I had known where they were going to send me, I would never have left the house at all. But it was too late now to undo anything.

If I'd known then how it would all turn out, I would've thrown myself on the ground, pleading and begging for them to give me one more chance. I would have tried even harder to be normal and not get into trouble or cause anyone any worry. But there wouldn't be any more chances for me now. I think somewhere, deep down, I always knew this day was coming, that it would finally get me. And now, here it was.

I sensed that this time was going to be different from the time when I was sent away before. This time, I was being sent away to the same place they had sent my mother just a few years ago, Alton State Hospital. There was no money left to send me to a regular hospital. Alton State Hospital was the place you were sent if you didn't have any money, the place you didn't come back from. I was scared, but also hopeful that I might get to see my mother. I knew that she was where they were sending me and maybe I would finally get to see her. I hadn't seen her since she'd been sent away, and no one understood how sad that made me. I was always asking someone to take me there and let me see her, but no one would.

Maybe deep down, I was hoping and wishing that someday I'd go there and finally get to be with my mother again. What I didn't understand is that a reunion with my mother, as much as I wanted it, wasn't important to anyone but me. What I also didn't understand is that just because you were in the same place as someone you loved didn't mean you'd ever get to see them.

On April 27, 1953, they took me away. Funny that I would always remember how the sun was shining that day. It was a beautiful spring day, and for years I would remember the way the sun felt on my face as it streamed through the back window of the sheriff's car. I knew that it was my last day of freedom. I wanted to scream and cry and jump out of the car. I wanted to run as far away as my legs would take me, but I felt frozen in my seat, unable to move no matter how hard I tried.

The sheriff drove me, along with my uncle and my grandmother, to the State Hospital. I remember them telling me I wouldn't have to stay very long.

"Rose, you will be able to come home as soon as you get better," my grandmother said. But I could hear the sadness in her voice. When I looked at her and our eyes met, she knew that I knew she was lying. I would never be coming back, but maybe she needed to believe that someday I might. Maybe that is what she needed to believe in order to bring me here. I wanted to believe it too.

"Will I get to see my mother?" I asked. "I know she'll want to see me." I couldn't understand why everyone was so quiet. Why wouldn't they answer me?

Finally, the sheriff spoke, "I don't know anything about your mother. Rose, please calm down and relax. We will be there soon enough. Then we'll see."

I didn't think I was acting upset, but I must've been because I could see that my grandmother was crying. I guess I had upset her again, just like I always did.

"Now, Rose," she said, "Please be quiet. I'm sure your mother is busy and may not be able to see you right away." But I knew my mother wouldn't be too busy to see me. Even if I sometimes had made her mad, she would still want to see me. I just knew she would.

I also knew I'd better try to be quiet. I tried to tell myself to calm down, just like they were telling me to do, but it was so hard. I could hear myself screaming in my head, *Let me out. Let me go,* but not a sound was coming out of my mouth. I wanted to jump out of the car and run to see my mother, or even run home. No one was going to let me do either one.

All I could think of was how soon I'd see my mother. I imagined that someone must have called ahead and told them I was coming, and she'd be waiting to see me. *How happy she must be,* I thought, *to know that I was coming to see her.* At least in all this darkness, the one bright spot would be seeing my mother.

Years later I would wonder if anyone had ever even told my mother that I was there. If they had, I know she would've been so glad to see me. Since we couldn't see each other, maybe it was for the best that they had never told her I was there. I know she would've wanted to see me, and us being kept apart would have made her sad, I think. Maybe the doctors thought it would have upset us too much to see each other, but I wanted so badly to see her.

Once again, just like so many other times in my life, I wasn't allowed to make a decision. Other people always controlled me. They had the power to decide what was best for me.

When we finally arrived at Alton State Hospital, the place that would now be my home, I was so surprised to see what it looked like. (Photo at right.) I'd always wanted to come here and visit my mother. No one would ever bring me, so I

Alton State Hospital in Alton, Illinois, where Rose was sent in 1953.

had imagined what it might look like. I could never have imagined how beautiful it was. It was like I was entering a magical city. There were so many buildings that I lost count. There were seven, maybe more, and some were very big. The main building looked like a magnificent castle, its massive windows peering out at me. For a minute I thought maybe I was Dorothy and they were taking me to the Wizard of Oz. I had seen that movie once. Maybe there really was someone who could fix what was wrong with me. Then I'd be all right, and everyone would want me to come back home. I was just like Dorothy in so many ways. We had so much in common. All we ever wanted to do was to find our way back home, but there were always so many things trying to stop us from getting there.

But there weren't any red ruby slippers I could wear and click together. No amount of chanting "There's no place like home, there's no place like home" would help me find my way back to my family. Maybe it's a good thing that I could never really remember what happened at the end of that movie. Maybe Dorothy never made it back home either. Maybe she lived all her life in the Land of Oz. Maybe.

My uncle and the sheriff got out of the car to walk me into the main building. My grandmother stayed in the car. I didn't know why she wasn't coming in with us. I looked back at her, and it looked like she was sobbing, her head cupped in her hands. I waved at her, but she didn't look up.

"I love you, grandmother, I'll see you soon," I yelled back at her, but she never looked up. I loved her very much and didn't want her to cry. Seeing her cry made me feel sad for all of us.

My uncle held onto my arm as we walked up the sidewalk. I could feel him shaking.

"Everything is going to be all right, Rose," I heard him say. I know he tried to sound convincing, but his voice was cracking and I didn't believe him. I could tell it was the main building we were walking up to because it was the biggest of all the buildings. It wasn't until the massive doors were opened and we were inside the building that I really got scared. As the doors closed shut behind us, a darkness started to fill up my whole body. It was like a nightmare that had always been waiting for me, waiting patiently to come true.

I could see the nurses as I got closer to the desk. I grabbed my uncle's arm, which was still shaking.

"Please don't leave me here, Uncle, please don't leave me here!" I could hear myself saying it over and over. I could hear myself getting louder and louder until finally I was screaming. I must have been screaming loud because some nurses came running, and everyone was telling me to calm down, telling me that everything would be all right.

"Rose, you have to be quiet. The other patients will get upset if they hear you screaming. You don't want to upset them. And you don't want to make yourself sick," my uncle said. *Sick,* I thought, *I'm already sick. That's why they brought me here. That's why they're leaving me here.*

I could hear my uncle saying goodbye and that everyone loved me and that I would get better, but I was screaming so loudly I was drowning his voice out. The nurses were pulling me down the hall, and my uncle had turned to leave.

"No," I screamed at him, "No, don't leave me here! Please! Please! I promise I will be better. Just please don't leave me here!" He kept on walking, his shoulders moving up and down as he went. I think he was sobbing like my grandmother had been, but I couldn't be sure.

"I promise I'll be better, just tell me what to do!" I screamed. "I'll die here, I'll die here. Please!"

I loved my uncle, but why was he leaving me here? I couldn't understand it. I think it was very hard for my uncle to have to bring me here, but the decision had been made. I think my family felt it was their only option, their only way to help me. I never saw my uncle again after that day, and watching him walk away, through my tears, I had to wonder if I would ever see any of my family again.

Chapter 8

Order of Commitment

My Petition for Commitment was filed in the Macoupin County courthouse in Carlinville, Illinois, on April 28, 1953. No time was wasted in having me legally committed. Since my mother had already been sent away and my father was dead, my grandmother was now my legal guardian. I imagine it was not easy for her to be the one to make the final decision to have me sent away, but she was getting older, and I'm sure she wondered who would care for me if something happened to her. As awful as it was to be me, I think it would've been far worse to be her and have to make the decisions she did. God granted her another decade on this earth after I was sent away, but I'm sure I was never far from her thoughts. I liked to think that this was an agonizing decision for my family. Maybe it's best that I never knew for sure.

On the day the Petition for Commitment was filed, it was ordered that two doctors were to act as a commission and examine me while I was in Alton State Hospital. Two doctors that I had never met before would decide my fate after spending all of one hour with me. One hour out of my life is all they would need in order to determine my future. For that moment in time, they exacted more control over my life than God Himself. At least I could pray to God; I couldn't do the same with these men. I knew their findings would seal my fate, and I was helpless to change the outcome. They had all the power. I had none.

On May 8, I was served papers letting me know that my commitment hearing would be held on May 14 at 1:30 p.m. at Alton State Hospital, which had now become my home. I never actually saw the papers, but I do remember someone telling me that a hearing would be held and that I would need to be there. How ironic that I was served papers informing me of my commitment hearing in the very place that they wanted to commit me to.

It was my receipt of these papers that rendered what they were doing legal and binding in the state of Illinois. It was at this hearing that the findings of the two doctors would be read. These findings would officially be called the Report of Commission, and it was this report the judge would use in order to render his decision about my fate. The rest of my life would now depend on the outcome of this one day, this one hearing. No one from my family would be there with me to hear what the decision would be.

On May 14, the day of the commitment hearing, I was brought to a room at Alton State Hospital that no doubt had seen many like me before. I didn't have far to travel since I'd been a patient at the hospital since April 27. Although I knew the chances were slim, I hoped there might be a small chance that the outcome of my hearing would mean that I would be sent home. Realistically, I knew that most likely wouldn't be the case. I was also hoping that someone from my family would be there, but I also knew the chances of seeing any of them were small. What I didn't realize then was that their faces were already becoming just a memory to me, and the memory was already beginning to fade.

The room was more pleasant that any of the other rooms I'd been in since I'd been at the hospital. The walls were at least a brighter shade of white than the faded paint of the rooms I'd been in. I was led to a chair by a nurse who helped me sit down behind a desk. She sat down next to me, and somehow that made me feel better. It was like someone was there for me, to support me and care about what happened to me. I could see another nurse standing by the door. There was also a man dressed in a white shirt and white pants. I had seen many men dressed like this since I had come to the hospital. I decided it must have been their uniform. Some of these men were nice; some were not.

I almost felt like a real person for a minute, like I was a real someone sitting behind that long desk. Then I realized what was happening. Everyone stood up when the judge walked in. The judge walked to the front of the room and sat down in a big wing-back chair behind a large wooden desk. We all sat down, too. His desk sat up higher than mine, and he had a lot of papers stacked in neat piles on his desk. I knew that this was someone important, someone people listened to.

It took all of 20 minutes for my fate to be sealed. The findings from the Report of the Commission, which was written by the two doctors who examined me only once, were read aloud. From that report, the judge determined that the Order of Commitment should be granted. His tone was sharp and cutting. This was not a man to question or to plead with. His decisions were final, and we all knew that.

When he was ready to speak, he motioned for me to stand up again. Clearing his throat for what seemed like forever, he finally began, "And it appearing to the court that the said Rose Ann Pianfetti is in Court in person as required by law and that due and proper notice of the time and place of hearing has been served upon all persons entitled thereto pursuant to the statute and the order of this Court. And this case now coming on to be heard upon the aforesaid petition and upon the finding of the Commission appointed by this Court, no demand having been made for jury and non-showing having been otherwise made that such a trial was necessary or desirable. In which the commission found that because of examination the said person is a mentally ill person incapable of managing and caring for her own estate."

It was the final words that I had yet to hear that would condemn me to the life that I could've only imagined in my worst nightmares. The judge cleared his throat again. "Now therefore, it is ordered on this 14th day of May, 1953, that the said Rose Ann Pianfetti be and is hereby adjudged to be a mentally ill person, incapable of managing and caring for her own estate. And it appearing to the court that the allegations in

said petition are true, it is ordered that said person be and is

hereby committed to the Department of Public Welfare for

admission to Alton State Hospital, Alton, Illinois, as provided in

in Sections 5-10 and 5-11 of the Mental Health Code."

And so it was read, my death sentence.

Chapter 9

Alton State Mental Hospital

After what seemed like days of crying in my room, I finally began to look around and see what my new life looked like, now that I wouldn't be leaving. It appeared that my new home was a city within a city. I discovered that there was a farm on the hospital grounds that produced all the food for the patients and staff. The farm produced not only fruits and vegetables, but milk, pork, beef, veal, corn, oats, hay and rye. Hogs and cattle were raised and then butchered for their meat. Vegetables were prepared and stored in the root cellar. In addition to a large laundry, the property held a bakery, canning facility, and many ice houses. Patients were allowed to work on the farm, in the bakery, or in the laundry if the staff felt they were capable. For many years, Alton State Hospital succeeded in meeting most of its patients' physical needs within its own walls and property. In the early 1950's, over 2,000 patients called Alton State Hospital home.

Each day, all three meals were served in the large dining hall. If a patient was not able to come to the dining room, their meal was delivered in cans and containers to their rooms. As for me, I ate many meals in my room, as I was too distraught to eat in the main dining hall. All the people made me nervous, and it was so loud that I couldn't hear myself think. It made me very anxious to be around so many people, and I would cry during most of my meal.

"What's the matter, Rose, why are you crying again?" one of the ladies would ask me. I couldn't answer though my tears. I just turned my head and tried to wipe my eyes.

"If you ain't gonna eat it, Rose, can I have your soup?" someone would inevitably say. "Be a shame to waste it."

I didn't care who took my food. I just wanted to be left alone. When I lifted my head and looked at my tray, my food would be gone. After a few times of my meals being eaten by other patients, the staff started bringing my meals to my room.

I think they thought I would eat if I was by myself with no one there to take my food. At least that way, I would eat something.

I never ventured far from my room. I never felt like talking. The doctors were always saying that I mumbled a lot and was always smiling to myself. The other patients made fun of me, but I didn't care. I found that I preferred sitting on the floor instead of a chair. They would tell me to get up and sit down on a chair like everyone else, but I wouldn't do it. I wanted to sit on the floor. Many times, I would lay on the floor until someone made me get up.

I would receive more shock therapy. Even though I had received eight treatments at St. Vincent's, which hadn't helped, the decision to give me more was probably made because the doctors didn't know what else to do. I soon discovered that ECT wasn't done the same way here. I wish it had been, because at least if you knew what to expect, you could brace yourself for what was coming.

When I heard the nurse say it was my turn for treatment, I felt sick to my stomach. Even though being at St. Vincent's had prepared me for what was to come, I had an awful feeling that this wasn't going to be the same. Things were done differently here at Alton State Hospital, and that included ECT.

I was led to a large room with many beds in it. Other patients lay in some of the beds while other beds were empty.

"Come on, Rose, let's lay down. Right here is a nice bed for you," one of the nurses said. That's when I realized that we'd all be in the same room while we got our therapy. I began to cry. My humiliation would now be shared with other people, and theirs with me.

I tried to fight a little at first, but not much, since I knew it wouldn't do any good. The nurse pulled me into the bed and clamped my arms and legs down. I could hear the clinking of the clamps and wanted to scream. *Couldn't the other patients see what was going on? Couldn't they try to help me?* Then I realized that they had all either received their shock treatment already or were going to receive it very soon. None could help me. They couldn't even help themselves.

At Alton, the shock cart was moved from bed to bed, and the patients were all given their treatments in front of each other. I heard screaming coming from the other end of the room. A patient was being given her treatment right in front of all of us. I couldn't believe it. We had to watch each other receive shock treatment. It felt like punishment, like something out of a House of Horrors. Perhaps we had all been bad and they were doing this to make us behave better. The lady in the next bed was shocked so hard that she had grand mal seizure movements with severe jerks. Her head was jerking so hard that I thought it would break her neck. I didn't scream or shout out, but I could feel the tears falling out of my eyes and running down my face. I wept for the other women and for myself. Then the nurse came up to my bed.

"Are you ready now, Rose?" I said no, but I knew it wouldn't matter. It was my turn, and there was nothing I could do to change that.

I didn't want to remember what had happened to me in that room full of women. It wouldn't be the last time I would be in that room or the last time that I would be strapped down. It would happen time and time again, until I no longer cared what became of me. That was the first time I remember no longer wanting to be me.

I spent five years at Alton State Hospital, one day melting into the next. Most of the time I didn't know what day or month it was. I tried to be a part of the institution's routine, but it was just too hard for me most days. It was easier not to talk when I was spoken to, since I always seemed to be in a fog. I thought it was just me, that my brain was all tumbled about, but I think it was all the medication they were giving me and the shock treatments. It was easier not to talk, and nothing I said ever made a difference anyway.

I do know that I waited every day for some word from my family. Even if no one came to visit me, I would've at least liked to know something about them, to hear something from them. I especially would've liked to know something about my mother. Was she still at Alton State Hospital, or had she gone home? I'd never know the answer. I

Galesburg State Research Hospital in Galesburg, Illinois, where Rose was transferred after her stay at Alton State Hospital.

was transferred to Galesburg State Research Hospital in 1958, and that is where I would spend the next 25 years before they moved me again. (See photo above.)

Chapter 10

The Bad Thing

I tried hard to hang on to some good memories to help me survive the long terrifying days of my existence. I would try as hard as I could to not remember the things that made me sad. More than anything, I tried not to remember the Bad Thing. The Bad Thing was the thing that everyone always said was part of the reason I was sent away. Sometimes, though, I can't think of anything else. The Bad Thing washes over me in bits and pieces until the memory of it makes me sick. I try not to think about it right before I go to bed. That's the worst time for me to remember. It often comes to me when I'm asleep, a nightmare that I know is real and that I'm afraid I can never wake up from. Thinking about that day scares me even when I am wide-awake.

I was twelve years old and was wearing my prettiest dress that day, the white one with the purple sash. I had tied my hair with my best bow. I knew it didn't look very pretty. It was always hard for me to do my hair by myself, but I was determined to look as nice as I could because this was a special day for me. I was going to go visit my friend Ruth.

I remember that it started out as a really nice day. The sun was shining, and the clouds were as white as snow. They were big and fluffy and reminded me of cotton candy. It felt like I could reach up and touch them if I wanted to. I didn't have time for that. I needed to concentrate on where I was going. I didn't get to go out a lot by myself, so I was lucky to get the chance to be out that day.

"Make sure you go straight to your friend's house, Rose, and come straight home when you're done. No stopping to talk to anyone," I heard my grandmother say. "You're always letting the time get away from you, you know." I was so excited to be able to go out by myself. I felt all grown up and free as a bird.

"Yes, I will," I said as I ran out the door. "I promise I'll come back home as soon as I'm done visiting."

I was so happy, being able to go all by myself to see Ruth. I was walking on one of the side streets because Grandmother didn't like me to walk on Main Street. She said I became too distracted by all the goings-on up on Main Street. I wasn't even sure what distracted meant, but I knew I needed to listen to her, so I used the side streets.

I tried my best to keep my thoughts on what I was doing, but I must not have been doing a very good job because when I heard his voice, it startled me. It came from behind me.

"Hello, Rose. Where are you going by yourself on this pretty day?" At first, I wasn't sure who it was.

"Oh, I'm just going to see my friend Ruth. My grandmother said I could go visit her today," I said.

"Well, that is mighty nice, I'd say." I was sure I knew his voice, knew who he was, but I couldn't quite place it. But I didn't like him walking behind me. It made me nervous. It seemed like I could feel his breath all over me. I started to walk faster.

"You sure look pretty today, Rose," he said. I turned around quickly to look at him, and I was right. I did know him. That is when I suddenly felt it, way down deep in the pit of my stomach, that feeling of knowing something wasn't right, a feeling of knowing I was in trouble. I knew he was not always a nice man. I started to feel afraid, but I didn't want him to see that I was scared of him.

I wasn't sure if I should answer the man. I thought I looked pretty today, too. But the way he said it to me made me feel funny in a bad way that I had never felt before. I hadn't been around many boys, so it was hard for me to know how to act. I decided to keep walking, hoping I might see someone else I knew. Now I wished I had been walking on Main Street where there were so many more people, maybe some people I could call out to and stop this man from following me.

"Oh, thank you," I said, hoping he couldn't tell how scared I was. "This is my favorite dress."

"Well, it sure looks nice on you. Oh, but look, your sash has come untied in the back. Why don't you stop a minute and let me tie it?" I froze. I knew my sash wasn't untied. I could feel it snug around my waist, just like when Grandmother had tied it before I left. I didn't know what to do. I felt like running, fast as I could, but my legs felt funny, and all I could do was keep trying to walk the best I could.

"Oh, never mind that sash," I said. "It doesn't bother me. It's always coming untied anyways," I lied.

He came up directly behind me, and I felt the sash come undone. I turned to tell him to please stop, but when I did, he placed his hand over my mouth and nose. I was so scared, I peed my panties. *Oh no,* I thought. It was so hard for me not to have an accident, and now I had really gone and done it. Pee was everywhere. I thought for sure it would stop the man, but he didn't seem to care at all. I thought about my pretty dress and how it would smell of pee now. Maybe Grandmother could get the smell out.

I couldn't breathe because he had his hand so tight over my mouth and nose. I struggled to break free, but his hand was big and he was strong. I couldn't get loose no matter how hard I tried.

"Don't fight, Rose," he said. "It will be over soon. The more you fight, the worse you'll make it." *What was he talking about? What will be over soon? What would I make worse?* I had no idea except that I knew it was something bad.

He yanked my head down and threw me in the ditch before climbing on top of me. He was so big I thought he would crush me and squish the air right out of me. Couldn't anyone see he was hurting me? But we were both lying in the ditch where no one could see us. Then I felt it ... the feeling of being torn in half. The pain was like nothing I had ever felt before. It felt like he was breaking me, and I almost passed out from the pain. What could I have done to make this man do this to me, to want to hurt me so bad? It was a question I would ask myself for the rest of my life. I struggled to stay conscious.

His hand slipped from my mouth, and I cried out for him to stop, but he didn't. He just covered my mouth again. His hand smelled of sweat and of my urine. That's when I started to cry. I knew I was crying because I could feel the tears streaming down my face. But there was no one to comfort me, and I was sure that I was going to die. Then I looked up and saw a cloud floating in the sky, a pretty cloud that I just started to stare at. I thought that as long as I didn't take my eyes off that cloud, I had a chance all of this might end soon.

It seemed like it took forever. When he was finally finished, he stood up. I turned my head aside so I didn't have to look at him. I was afraid to look at him, afraid he might hurt me again. His eyes darted around. Then he told me to run home and not to tell anyone if I knew what was good for me. He looked around again and then took off running.

I was so happy he was gone, but I was afraid to move. When I was sure he was gone, I turned my head and looked up to the sky. *How could this have happened?* I wondered. I was all dressed in my pretty dress to go and play with my friend. What had I done to make this happen? Even though I was looking at the blue sky and the pretty white clouds, I felt sick. I knew that nothing was ever going to be the same again.

When I finally stood up and started to pull up my panties, I saw there was blood. I thought I must be dying, there was so much blood. I worried that Grandmother would be so mad at me. I pulled my dress down and saw that it was covered in dirt, grass stains, and blood. *Oh no, no, no, I will be in so much trouble. My favorite dress is ruined, and it's all my fault.* I started to cry again.

I tried my best to run home, but I could hardly see through my tears, and it hurt so bad that I could only walk. I walked as fast as I could, but it was hard because I was crying and trying not to fall down.

It felt like it took forever to get home. When I came through the back door into the kitchen, my grandmother was there.

"Rose, you're back so soon. Wasn't your friend home?" I was so glad to be home that I ran to her, but I stumbled and fell down.

"Oh, my goodness, Rose, let me help you. What happened? And your dress? It's torn, and what is that? Is that blood? Stop your crying and tell me what happened."

My grandfather came in then and picked me up, then carried me upstairs to my bed.

"My Lord, what happened to you, Rose, please tell us!" I was afraid to tell them. I knew they would be upset with me and think it was all my fault.

"You have to tell us, Rose, or we won't know how to help you."

So I told them. I could see that they were both crying. I wondered why. They hadn't done anything wrong. After I finished telling them, my grandmother could hardly look at me, and I was afraid she was mad at me, but then I realized she was trying not to let me see that she was crying.

"It's all right, Grandmother, I'm ok now, I'm home. It's all right. It's all my fault, but I'm home now."

I couldn't get out of bed for two days. My grandparents took care of me and never, not then or ever, talked to me about what the bad man had done. I could tell they didn't want me to talk about it either, so I didn't. I would live the rest of my life thinking that the bad thing was my fault, and that I had somehow caused it.

Chapter 11

Going Home

I was discharged from Galesburg State Hospital in 1983 due to its impending closure in 1985. I was sent to so many different nursing homes there was no way I could keep track of them even if I was able to. It was an endless string of lonely nursing home rooms with no hope of anything changing for me. Other patients would have family come to visit them, but not me. By the end, I had given up hope of ever seeing anyone from my family again here on this earth. I didn't live; I existed. Day after day. I became a broken woman in body, but never in spirit, as I knew that one day I would find a way to get home. Perhaps not in this life, but I had learned long ago that you must believe in something bigger than yourself, something that will give you the strength to at least keep breathing.

I knew that when I died, no one from my family would know. I had been declared a ward of the state long ago. I had no idea what would happen when I died, but I also knew that I had to somehow be with my family again. I had questions that I had never gotten answers for. Was my mother dead? Had my brother married? Did he have any children? Was he alive? It broke my heart to think that I would never know what had happened to the people that I had loved so long ago. Years before, their faces and voices had begun to fade in my memories, as I was now an old woman. At 73, my body looked and felt much, much older due to the institutionalized life I had lived.

One day, after being sent to the hospital, God called me home. I was happy to finally be set free. No more lonely rooms, no more endless pills, no more simply existing. I was taken to a funeral home and was buried in a potter's field. No family, no headstone, no flowers. Just a number assigned by the state for the rest of eternity.

But this was not to be the way it would end for me. I wanted to go home, to be buried next to my mother, the mother that I had loved and longed for. I wanted to rest between her and my grandmother. Yes, I wanted to go home. I had always prayed the day would come when I would see my home again. This is where my story on earth ends and my journey home begins. Finally, after waiting a lifetime, I was going home.

Part II: Finding Rose; Bringing Her Home

In 1971, when I was eight years old, my grandmother asked me if I knew where her daughter Rose was and what had happened to her. Even as a young girl, I could see the deep sadness in my grandmother's eyes when she asked me about her daughter, Rose. I couldn't give her an answer because I didn't know, but I would never forget what she asked me. This is the story of how I was finally able to get the answers to the questions my grandmother asked of me so many decades ago. This is the story of how I found my Aunt Rose Ann Pianfetti and brought her home to rest with her family.

Chapter 1

Family Secrets

Some of us are prisoners to a past we didn't participate in. Even though we had no say in the decisions that were made, we had to live with the consequences of those decisions. My family had a secret that had to be protected because it was shameful. The power of this secret, the committal of my Aunt Rose to a state mental hospital when she was only 17 years old and the events leading up to that day, grew stronger as the years unfolded. My journey of finding and bringing my aunt home taught me that secrets can alter the course of a family for generations to come. My family's secret set in motion a series of events that would forever change the lives of all those involved. I've learned that a person never truly knows what they are capable of until faced with a life-changing decision.

Families didn't talk out loud about people like Rose. They whispered. They kept her existence a secret and only talked about her in hushed tones. I was eight years old when I first heard her name. It would be years before I would know the full extent of the secret and the price my family paid for keeping it. Rose was a person, flesh and blood, long exiled from her family. She would wait over 56 years to finally come home and break the chains of guilt and shame that held her captive.

Growing up, I heard vague whisperings about her, hushed tones that would abruptly end as I walked into a room.

"Rose was just never right," I would hear a muffled voice saying. "You know, she was always getting in trouble for something. And then after that thing happened, I mean, what else could have been done? She had to be sent away." As a young girl, I didn't understand what they were talking about, but I understood enough to know to not ask any questions. So no questions were asked, and the secret about my Aunt Rose remained safe.

It wasn't as if there weren't enough other worries to keep my family occupied. There were plenty. Rose's mother, Helen, who was my grandmother, spent most of her adult life in and out of state mental institutions after her husband had her committed to Alton State Hospital in 1948. In 1969, when I was six years old, she was discharged and came to live with us. In the early 1970's, the deinstitutionalization movement had begun in mental institutions in the United States, fueled in part by an article in the *New York Times* in September 1965. The article quoted then-US Attorney General Robert Kennedy as saying that the conditions at a New York state mental institution called Willowbrook were like a "snake pit." A place like this is where my grandmother spent a large portion of her adult years and where Rose spent nearly all her life.

Growing up with someone who spent almost her entire adult life in and out of state mental institutions had a profound effect on me. Although our life was difficult at times, I learned to have empathy for those who struggle with mental illness. My grandmother was diagnosed with manic depression, but today it's known as bipolar disorder. She was also probably suffering from severe clinical depression. Her formal education had ended after the seventh grade, and her first marriage ended in divorce, not a common occurrence for a woman in the 1940's, which placed her at an even greater disadvantage.

I believe that Rose's traumatic birth and my grandmother's inability to mother Rose effectively set the stage for her disastrous second marriage. When she started to exhibit signs of depression by crying uncontrollably and acting nervously, her second husband, Rose's stepfather, found it all too easy to have her committed, even though she was the one who owned the house they lived in. I was surprised to learn how easily a husband could have his wife committed in the 1940's. Today, a woman diagnosed with bipolar disorder is treated so much differently than my grandmother was over 60 years ago. In her case, it took little more than the husband initiating the commitment process. Even the initial intake interview showed that the staff questioned her husband's motives, but ultimately decided to base their judgements on everything he said.

My grandmother began to exhibit more pronounced signs of mental illness after being subjected to numerous shock treatments in Alton State Hospital. I think she gave up at some point and just did the best she could to survive in that place, as her own daughter would also have to learn to do just four years later. Even though Rose would be sent to the same state institution as her mother, they would never see each other there. I'm sure Rose was hoping they would. The fact that they were at the same place and never laid eyes upon each other is a heartbreaking irony. While Rose was at Alton State Hospital, I'm sure she wondered if her mother was there. What Rose didn't know was that her mother was discharged in 1956, re-admitted in 1957, and then discharged again later that year. Although my grandmother was in and out of Alton State Hospital many times, Rose would never get the opportunity to leave the many institutions in which she would spend her entire life. Even though Rose was committed to Alton State Hospital in 1953, she spent most of her life in Galesburg State Research Hospital. The hospital had opened in 1949 and not only provided treatment and care for the mentally ill, but also served as a center for the study of mental illness. Rose was transferred to Galesburg from Alton in March 1958 and would live there until December 1983.

I'm not sure why Rose was transferred to Galesburg, but it appears from her mental health records that she was becoming somewhat aggressive and combative. One can only imagine that no matter what other problems she may have had, Rose was most certainly feeling angry and confused at being taken to Alton State Hospital. It's easy to understand why Rose would have felt abandoned by her family. Once the days began to turn into weeks, then into months, and finally into years, with no one coming for her, I think Rose just gave up.

The fact that the Galesburg State Research Hospital's name included the word "research" gives me reason to wonder if Rose was subjected to any treatment besides the numerous electric shock therapy treatments that I do know she received. She may not have been, since the research hospital studied mainly problems of the older mentally ill population, but I'll never know for sure. By the time Rose was transferred there, she would have been considered a "ward of the state," and I'm not sure how her consent to be involved in research studies would have been obtained. In the 1950's, the consent process would've been much different than the process we have come to expect now. Today, Rose would have been considered a member of a "vulnerable population," but that might not have been the case then. Since she was a ward of the state with no family to intercede on her behalf, would she have been considered an easy target as a research participant? We'll never know if Rose was involved in any research at all during her many years at Galesburg, but the chances are pretty good that she might have been.

In 1983, Galesburg State Research Hospital was preparing for closure, so Rose was transferred. The transfer would send her to the first of many different nursing homes where she would spend the next 25 years of her life. She was transferred so frequently that it's hard to follow her tracks, even when reading her records. She spent a great deal of time in isolation due to her bouts of aggression and non-compliance. She often became angry and lashed out at some of the other patients by pulling their hair. She would also try to take food from the other patients' trays. Many institutions had, at one time, used food as a tool for behavior control. Maybe that explained why Rose was always trying to steal food. Maybe she was always afraid she wouldn't have enough to eat.

I was told that one of the reasons for Rose's many transfers in the state mental system is that she would have been sent wherever there was a bed available. Rose became a ward of the state soon after she was committed, so she would have been at the bottom of the list regarding where she was sent. When I found Rose, I was able to travel and see the last place she had lived in and meet with her caretakers. I so badly wanted them to know that this person they had thought had no one did, in fact, have a family. She was someone; she mattered. I thanked them for caring for her and took them a copy of the only picture I had of Rose as a young girl. I wanted them to see that this grown woman, who had no hope of ever leaving the system she had been sentenced to, was once a young girl who had hopes and dreams. She was a somebody. She had a family. She was loved.

Chapter 2

Understanding the Past

My father never spoke of Rose. I have often wondered why he chose to never share anything about her. The truth was that they didn't really grow up together. Before being sent to Alton State Hospital, Rose lived with her grandparents, except for the two years that she lived with her mother and stepfather. Six months of that time, she was sent away to the sanitarium in Springfield. I think as my father was growing up, he saw that Rose was different and all too easily assumed that she must've had the same mental health problems as their mother, or something similar. What we know now, and what no one understood then, is that before the 1940's, children who are now called autistic were given the label of psychotic, schizophrenic, or emotionally disturbed. If Rose did have autism, as I believe she may have, she had the misfortune of being born in the Age of Denial of autism, which defined the 1940's – 1960's.

108

Many of the behaviors that Rose exhibited both before and after she was committed in 1953 make a strong case for the fact that Rose may have been a child with autism. Often in her records, Rose is frequently described as presenting with echolalia, which is a condition where a child continuously repeats words he or she has heard. Rose's need for things to be done a certain way, such as redoing household chores and her need to keep a book with long lists of things that were important to her, are other characteristics of children with autism.

It wasn't until 1964, with the publication of Bernard Rimland's book, *Infantile Autism: The Syndrome and Its Implications for a Natural Theory of Behavior,* that the similarities in the behavior of brain-injured children and autistic children were even considered. If this shift in thinking regarding autism had been known and understood when Rose was born in 1934, her life might have been much different. Her traumatic birth no doubt led to brain damage as she was being yanked and pulled from her mother's womb. The severity of this damage was something Rose would have to live with and something no one would understand or be able to help her with. Rose was one of many children born in a time and to a generation of people who were ill equipped to help her. Rose's family dynamics were not strong, which didn't help her either. Perhaps if her father hadn't died and her mother hadn't had multiple issues to deal with, including manic depression, Rose's life could have been much better.

New research from recent studies has shown that a relationship may exist between breech births and autistic tendencies. The research brings up the possibility of whether autistic tendencies in the fetus may lead to breech presentations. The research is showing not so much a causation between the two factors, but that there may be a relationship between the two.

To be honest, finding Rose was not something I had set out to do in the fall of 2009. Years earlier, in the mid-1990's, I had tried unsuccessfully to locate Rose. Someone had said Rose might be a patient in a mental institution in a nearby city. I called this institution but was told that no one by the name of Rose Pianfetti had ever been a patient there. It wasn't true. Though Rose wasn't there when I called, she had been a patient there previously, for almost a year. A private investigator told me that without a social security number, finding Rose would be next to impossible. Since she hadn't been issued one until after she was committed, there was no way of knowing what it was.

Later I was told that even if Rose had been at that institution when I called, I probably wouldn't have been told she was there. Since she was a mental patient and a ward of the state, refusal to tell me she was there would've been seen as protecting her rights. As unfair as it seems, I apparently was not supposed to find my aunt at this point.

I harbor no illusions about what I could or would have done had I found Rose back then. I know I couldn't have brought her home to live with me. My husband and I were raising our three children at the time, and I know I couldn't have brought her into my home to live with my family then.

Maybe I could've had her moved to a place closer to where I lived. I could've visited her and made sure she had what she needed. I could've made sure that her caretakers knew she had a family who loved and cared about her. But most importantly, Rose would have known that she was loved. I would've told Rose that when her grandmother was interviewed all those years ago by the staff at Alton State Mental Hospital, she'd told them that the family wanted Rose to come home again, when she was able. Rose would've known that her family had wanted her to come back home, that they loved her. But it was not to be. I would never get to tell her these things while she walked on this earth. It is one of my greatest regrets.

Chapter 3

Searching for Rose

In the fall of 2009, my daughter decided to sign up for a trial of Ancestry.com so she could learn more about our family. Because of an email my daughter sent through the Ancestry.com website, she received a response from someone who turned out to be my second cousin. When my daughter decided to meet with this relative, I asked her to find out if he knew anything about Rose and what may have happened to her. Since he was older than I, I hoped he might know something about her. Not surprisingly, although the meeting went well, he didn't know where Rose might be. I didn't think much more about it, since I wasn't really expecting him to know anything.

He decided to run her name through Ancestry, which is how he discovered Rose's death record. The death record contained her social security number and date of death. When

113

he sent it to me, I cried for days. She had died on January 14, 2009, just nine months earlier. I had missed finding her by only nine months! I couldn't believe it. I had never dreamed my aunt would have lived 56 years in mental institutions and nursing homes. I had assumed she would have passed away years ago. My father died when he was just 44, and my grandmother died when she 60. Who would have ever thought that Aunt Rose would have stayed alive until she was 73? I knew then, deep in my heart, that she had been waiting, holding on for her family to find her and bring her home. But we had failed her. She had died, and I had no idea where she was buried or even whom to contact to find out.

That is when my real search for my Aunt Rose began. I had to find her, to know where she was, where she had been, and where she was buried. I contacted the Social Security office and was told that they couldn't give me any information about her, even though I knew her social security number and date of death. I decided to just start making phone calls, starting with the city of Galesburg since that was the last state institution she had been in. I called the coroner, hospitals, and nursing homes. Although I was able to find out that she had been treated at some area hospitals, it had only been for blood work or minor procedures. After spending four days on the phone, I was no closer to finding her than when I'd started.

I really needed to find the city where she had died in order to find her. I decided to call the Social Security office one more time and see if someone might decide to help me. I think angels were working a little overtime that day. When I made the call and again was told that they couldn't help me, something in my voice when I responded must've made the person on the other end decide to do the right thing. My voice cracked as I explained that my aunt was dead, and all I wanted was to find out where she was buried.

Then I heard the two words that would change everything and help me finally find my aunt. Rock Island. I wasn't sure I had heard right. There were a few seconds of silence, then I heard the words, "Did you hear me?"

"Yes. Yes, I heard you. Thank you so much," I said. "I can't tell you what this means to me." It was my first concrete lead toward finding my aunt. That person will never know how grateful I will always be for that seemingly small piece of information that changed everything.

Chapter 4

Rose is Found

When I started making phone calls again, things went much better than before. I called the coroner in Rock Island, and yes, he had a death record for Rose. Tears ran down my face as I wrote down everything he was saying. He was even able to tell me the nursing home Rose had been in and the funeral home that her body was sent to. I couldn't believe my ears. I had found her! I would soon be talking to the people who would be able to tell me exactly where she was.

As happy as I was that I was getting so close to finding my aunt, I was also a little scared of what I might discover. What would these people think of a family who never came to visit their family member? I felt a great deal of sadness that Rose's family, my family, had never been able to visit her. I will carry that regret with me for the rest of my life. There was nothing I could do to change anything about the past, but I could continue this journey and find Rose and bring her home at last.

I called the funeral home first to see if Rose had been taken there. I held my breath as the phone began ringing. When I heard the voice on the other end of the line, I could hardly speak. "I'm calling to find out if a Rose Pianfetti was brought to your funeral home."

After a few minutes of silence that felt like hours, she answered, "Why yes, we did conduct that funeral. Would you like to speak to the gentleman that handled it?" I was afraid that I hadn't heard her correctly. Finally, I was going to talk to someone who could really help me find my aunt! I held it together and said, as calmly as I was able, "Yes, please, that would be really helpful."

The next thing I knew, a kind voice greeted me on the other end of the phone. "May I help you? I understand you are inquiring about a Rose Pianfetti, is that correct?"

"Yes, it is," I answered. "She was my aunt."

"Oh, we were under the impression that Ms. Pianfetti had no family." There it was. No family. She had no family. That's what they all would think. But it wasn't true.

"No, she had family," I said as I choked back the tears. "I am her family. Are you able to tell me anything? I've been looking for her. I can't believe I've finally found her."

"She was brought here from the hospital," he said. "Her state-appointed guardian said that she had no family, so the burial was a state funeral. We ran her death notice in the local paper three times, but no one came forward."

"Of course not," I said, "she wasn't from there. None of her family lives there." I had so many questions I wanted to ask.

"Is she buried in the local cemetery?"

"Yes, she is. I performed the small service here at the funeral home and then oversaw the simple arrangements at

119

the cemetery." I couldn't believe I was finally finding out what had happened to my Aunt Rose. What I didn't realize at the time was that this man would prove to be a guardian angel for my Aunt Rose and for me.

I asked the first thing that popped into my head. "So, if she is buried in the cemetery, can a headstone be put there?" There was a slight silence, and I don't think anything could have prepared me for what he was going to say next.

"Well, no, you can't, Mrs. Eccher, she is buried in a potter's field. You can't put a headstone in a potter's field." I felt a sudden pain, that quick, sharp punch in the stomach that you don't see coming. It took my breath away, and I couldn't speak for what seemed like an eternity.

"Mrs. Eccher, are you there? Did you hear me?"

Even though I was in a daze, the words I would say next were the most determined I had ever uttered.

"My aunt will NOT be staying in a potter's field. She is my family, my blood, and I don't care what it takes, or how much it costs, but I will be getting her out of there and bringing her home to Mt. Olive. She will be buried by her mother and grandmother, in her hometown, where she belongs."

As I spoke the words, I had no idea how I would make any of this happen. I also didn't have a lot of money to make sure it did. But I knew I'd find a way. What I did know is that I had finally found my aunt, who had waited 56 long and horrifying years to come home. I would bring her home, no matter what it took. She was my family, and she belonged with us.

"Mrs. Eccher, we've never exhumed someone from a potter's field before. That has never been done here." Hearing those words only made me more determined.

"It will be done now," I answered. "My aunt is coming home. So, where do we start? What do I need to do?"

"I honestly don't know; I'll have to talk with the cemetery caretaker and see what we can do."

"Thank you," I said. "I appreciate that. I'll do whatever you need me to do." That's what began a phone relationship with a man I had never met, talking about exhumations, graves, and cremation, a man who heard me cry so many times I can't even count, who listened patiently to a woman I'm sure he thought had lost her mind and who heard me beg for any details he could remember. Truth be told, he was one of the many angels God would put in place to help me bring Rose home.

It was almost a week before I heard back from him. It was not good news. Since an exhumation had never been done at the potter's field, the cemetery caretaker didn't feel comfortable doing one now. Since the caretaker couldn't be forced to perform the exhumation, there would need to be a board meeting to decide what to do. That wouldn't happen for another two weeks. My heart and head were racing. I let it be known that I was prepared to come there and perform the exhumation myself, if necessary. I understood that this would be highly unorthodox, but everyone needed to understand that my aunt was not staying there. She was coming home, and I would do everything and anything in my power to make that happen. I meant it; I would get a lawyer if I had to. Since my aunt had no children, I was her closest living relative. I would fight to make this happen. I would contact the local media and tell her story and do whatever I had to do to get her out of there and bring her home. I was told it was best that I didn't attend the meeting, so all I could do was wait for their decision.

While I waited to hear the verdict of the board, I decided to contact the funeral director in Mt Olive. Ed Becker's family had run the funeral home in Mt. Olive for decades. Ed had taken over the funeral home from his father who had taken it over from his father before him. You must be a special person to know how to offer comfort to the people of your own town when you bury their family members, and Ed was this special

123

person. I knew he would be able to let me know what had to be done on my end to be able to bring my aunt home. He told me that since my aunt had been buried in January, we would need to do the exhumation before winter.

"If we have to wait until next spring for the exhumation, I don't know if that is something that can be done," Ed said. "You have my full support, and this is do-able if it's done very soon, especially since it's now November. And please let the other funeral director know he can call me if he has any questions."

Ed's support made all the difference. The funeral director did call Ed, and I think it helped immensely that we had Ed on our end making sure things got done. Ed also helped me understand why Rose might have been sent away. He said that many children born with physical disabilities or autism were sent to institutions in the 1940's. Families did what their doctors told them to do. I hadn't done any research yet, so hearing this helped me understand that perhaps Rose being sent away was what happened when families didn't know how to cope. It was a different time.

I was on pins and needles, waiting for the call to let me know what the board had decided. I'd made up my mind that no matter what the decision, I would figure out a way to have my aunt's body exhumed, cremated, and brought home to Mt. Olive to be buried. It would, however, be so much easier if the cemetery board would agree to do it.

When he called, I couldn't tell from his voice whether it was good news or bad news. "Well, the good news is that the board agreed that legally you have the right to do this. They can't stop you. This is your aunt, and you are her blood relative," he said. "They just have never done this before. I did explain to them the time crunch we are under, and they seem willing to cooperate."

"What is the bad news?" I asked. "I can tell from your voice there is something else."

"Yes," he said. "They feel they will need to double the charge for this since it isn't something they've ever done."

Doubling the price was not the end of the world. The main thing was that they were going to do it. I was not anticipating this, but the truth is, I would've paid anything to bring her home. I would've begged, borrowed, or stolen for her if I had to. Then I learned I wouldn't have to.

He continued, "I've talked to the owner of our funeral home, and he has agreed to lower our cost, so that it can somewhat make up for the extra on the cemetery fees." I couldn't believe it. What a decent, kind thing to do. I was speechless.

"Are you there?" he asked.

"Yes, I'm here. That is so very kind. I can't even begin to thank you for all you're doing."

"Well, quite honestly, we've never had anything like this happen before, and we want to help in any way we can. There is just one thing, before we start this whole process. Are you totally sure you don't want to just leave your aunt where she is, now that you have found her?"

Hesitating, I finally answered, "My aunt waited 56 years for someone to come and bring her home. But no one came for her. Until now. I found her or she found me, I'm not sure which. But we found each other. What I couldn't do for her in life, I can do for her in death. I hope I can give her soul peace by bringing her home where she belongs, with her family, back to her town. I can't live with myself if I don't do this. I need to know that she will forever rest with her mother and grandmother."

"Well, all right," he said. "Then let's get started."

Chapter 5

Rose Comes Home

Impatiently, I waited for the day of the exhumation. It had to be done on a day with no snow or ice and coordinated with the funeral home and cemetery. The crematorium also needed to be available so that my aunt's body could be taken directly there. I had considered traveling to be present for the exhumation, but decided against it, as I didn't want to become emotional and interfere with the work that needed to be done. Instead, I kept my phone with me, waiting for updates of the progress.

I had asked if it would be possible to obtain a lock of hair from my aunt. A family member had suggested this. It could be a way to confirm beyond a doubt that it was indeed my aunt that was being exhumed. A lock of her hair could be checked for DNA and compared to my DNA if we ever needed to confirm that it was indeed Rose. It also would be something that was hers, something that I would know was hers for me to have, something tangible that I could hold in my hand, that would prove to me that I'd found her, my dad's sister. I asked the funeral director, and he assured me he would do his best to obtain a lock of her hair.

The funeral director checked in every few hours to let me know that progress was being made and that things were moving along. I knew that performing the exhumation wouldn't be an easy task. All I really knew about a potter's field was that those buried there are poor, without known family, and many times unidentified. What I learned is that potter's fields go back to the times of the Bible. I should have known this, I guess, for there always have been people who have been poor, and for whatever circumstance, lost to their families.

Potter's field is of biblical origin,[1] referring to a ground where clay was dug for pottery, later bought by the high priests of Jerusalem for the burial of strangers, criminals and the poor.

The term comes from Matthew 27:3-27:8 in the New Testament of the Bible, in which Jewish priests take 30 pieces of silver returned by a remorseful Judas:

Then Judas, who betrayed him, seeing that he was condemned, repenting himself, brought back the thirty pieces of silver to the chief priests and ancients, saying: "I have sinned in betraying innocent blood." But they said: "What is that to us? Look thou to it." And casting down the pieces of silver in the temple, he departed, and went and hanged himself with a halter. But the chief priests, having taken the pieces of silver, said: "It is not lawful to put them into the corbona, because it is the price of blood." And after they had consulted together, they bought with them the potter's field, to be a burying place for strangers. For this the field was called Haceldama, that is, the field of blood, even to this day.

I was told that the crematorium was available, so my aunt's body would be taken directly there once she was exhumed. The cremation would take place that day or the next.

My mind couldn't even travel to that part yet. I just wanted to hear that the exhumation had happened and that it was complete. The next phone call let me know that they had completed their work at the cemetery, and my aunt was on her way to the crematorium.

It hadn't been an easy job since the funeral director only had one other person helping him. It took the better part of the day to complete the exhumation. On that day he helped my aunt leave her potter's grave and get one step closer to coming home. I can never repay him for this.

"She is on her way to the crematorium and is no longer, in any way, a part of the potter's field cemetery," the funeral director said in his final call. "I do need to tell you, though, that the number she was assigned when she was buried here at the potter's field will always stay as her number."

"That's fine," I said, "it doesn't matter, because my aunt no longer has any use for it."

131

"Oh, and one more thing," he said. "I wasn't able to get a lock of her hair. I am so sorry." I was silent for a moment. I had so wanted that lock of hair, just for confirmation, just so no one could question whether it was my aunt or not, but I totally understood.

"That's all right," I said. "I want to thank you so much for trying. You did so much for my family today."

"But, wait," he said, "I did get something else."

What could he have gotten, I wondered? My aunt owned nothing, had nothing, so what could he possibly have gotten from her?

"It was her hospital bracelet," he said. "It was still on her wrist when she was buried. I cut it off, and I have it for you."

I tried to take in the words I was hearing. He had her wrist band from the hospital. It would have her name on it, her birth date. It was hers. She had worn it. This was it. This was the sign that I had dared not hope for but was secretly praying for. I knew now, without a shadow of a doubt, that this was my Aunt.

My Aunt Rose! She had found a way, in her death, even across time, to let me know that I had found her. There could be no

doubt now. I had found my aunt and she was coming home. (Photo at left.)

The hospital bracelet on Rose's wrist when she was buried in potter's field, which was recovered during her disinterment.

I received a call when the cremation was completed. We needed to set up a day that I would come and collect my aunt's ashes and bring her home. On my end, I had to set up details with Ed and the funeral home in Mt Olive. It was hard to believe I was at this point. Being able to physically bring my aunt home to rest with her family was the only thing I could do for her now. I hoped that this one thing would bring peace to not only her, but to my grandmother and great-grandmother as well. Knowing she would rest with them forever was the only thing I could do for these brave, wounded women. I could only be so lucky in my life to have a fourth of the courage these women had shown in their lifetimes. Words cannot express how grateful I am to have their DNA imprinted on my heart and soul.

Picking up my aunt's ashes proved to be bittersweet. As happy as I was to be bringing her home, I still felt great sadness that I never got to meet her. But getting to meet the funeral director who had done so much for us and thanking him in person was very healing. He was such a blessing to my family. I will never forget all he did to help bring Rose home. Without his help, her journey home wouldn't have happened.

Ed needed to take me to the cemetery to show me where my family's burial lots were. I knew where my great-grandparents, grandmother, and great-uncle were buried, but I had no idea that my family owned ten lots. Since only four had been used, there were, of course, six left.

"I really want her to be buried between her mother and grandmother, Ed. Is that possible?" I asked.

Ed pondered this, and I was so hopeful that he could make it work.

"Since we are burying her ashes, I think we could. We should be able to bury her right between them, and there would be room for a headstone. You wouldn't even be using a lot, so you would still have six left."

That was exactly what I was hoping for, that Rose would be able to rest forever right between the two women that she so loved.

I wish I had known years ago that my family had these lots. My father could have been buried there, but I now know that my family didn't talk about the difficult things. My father had never brought me to these family burial lots. I found where my family was buried years after he died. I remember seeing the headstone of my great-grandmother's and thinking, *There she is, the woman I am named for, Anna Caroline.* Since then, I had been coming to visit them and putting flowers on their graves. I was grateful to God that I was led to them so that, one day, I would know where to bring Rose.

"This is perfect, Ed, Rose buried right between them so her spirit will rest forever with the women that came before her. Yes, that is exactly what I want for her."

"Okay," said Ed. "Then I'll get started with the arrangements."

I had spent many years blaming the ghosts of my family for what happened to Rose. It took me a long time to understand that the time she lived in greatly decided her fate. Rose lived during a time when people with developmental delays and mental issues were subjected to severe treatments and institutionalization with little hope for their recovery. But Rose was finally home now and would be buried with her family, the family that loved her and, I have come to believe, did the best they could for her at the time.

Now that I knew where Rose would be buried, I could work on finalizing plans for the funeral. I wanted very much to give Rose a funeral with a full church service, including a choir, procession to the cemetery, and a dinner after. It happened due to the actions of many kind and caring people who helped me to make Rose's funeral her homecoming. I will never be able to express my complete thanks to all those who helped me. Ed kindly donated the funeral home's services, and Zion Lutheran Church will forever hold a special place in my heart, for it is where Rose's funeral was held. We celebrated her life there, and I know she heard us singing and thanking God for her.

The following is the eulogy I wrote for Rose's funeral:

I would like to thank everyone who has come today to help us celebrate Rose's homecoming. It means a lot to our families. A special thank you to Ed for his help and encouragement through this journey. Thank you for helping Rose to have this special day. Your help will never be forgotten. Thank you to the choir, what an amazing group of people. Thank you for giving Rose music today.

We are gathered together today to say goodbye to our Aunt

Rose, a woman who most people here have never met. We have

this picture of Rose when she was a young girl that shows her

with her brother and

with her arm around

her mother. (Photo at

right.) This was a

family, a family that

loved one another, no

Family portrait, from left: Dominic, Helen, and Rose Pianfetti.

matter what heartache would later come their way, they were a

family.

We do know that Rose had a nickname when she was little,

she was called "Rosie." We also know that Rose was named for

her father's mother, Rosa Pianfetti. This was most definitely a

child that was loved and wanted.

Through the years only vague whispers of Rose were spoken,

in hushed tones. All we really knew was that she had been sent

away when she was young and that no one talked about it. What we have come to know is that Rose had the misfortune of having a mental illness in a time when mental illness meant institutionalization. The medical minds of the 1950's believed that placing a person in a state mental institution was the only way for the family to cope with the problem. It would be accurate to say that Rose's only crime was of being born in the wrong generation. There was no medication for her illness, and no one in her family knew how to help her. They just did the best that they could.

In order to understand just how brave Rose was, I would like us all to try and envision the following scenario. You are seventeen years old, you are scared, you know that you are sick, but you don't know what is wrong. There is no medication to help you, no counseling services available, and there are some people that have hurt you and you don't understand why. Now, you are taken to a strange, scary place and left there with no family, no friends. Days turn into months, months turn into years,

years now turn into decades, you want to go home, but that never happens. So how do you survive this?

The truth is, I assumed Aunt Rose must have died long ago, surely no one could have lived all those years in the awful state mental institutions that we subjected patients to. But I was wrong, not only did she live, but she lived fifty-six years in conditions that most of us probably can't imagine. What a brave and strong woman this was, to live all those years being moved from one institution to another and surviving, always, always waiting to come home.

Today, I would say to her great nieces and nephews, that when you think of this woman, this woman that you never met, think of her with pride, be so proud of her. Proud of her courage and her strength, because these are gifts that she has given to you. Her spirit walks with you and because of you, she will not be forgotten. You will keep her memory alive in the years to come as you one day tell your own children about this very brave woman.

The journey to bring Rose home began very simply, with my children wanting to find out more about our family's history by going to Ancestry.com. And that led to meeting a cousin. We are forever grateful to that cousin for finding out that Rose had passed in time for us to be able to bring her home. Had another year gone by, we would not be sitting here today. When I was told that Rose was buried in a potter's field, it broke my heart. I knew immediately that my father's sister, my aunt, could not rest there. No matter what it took, she would be coming home. And although we hit a few rough turns, God and Rose worked it out so that this day could happen. Aunt Rose deserved to be moved one more time, we owed her that much, at least. She deserved to finally get the last move she had waited for all her life, the move that would bring her home to us.

As much as our hearts break for what Rose had to endure, and as much as we would like to, as much as I would like to, we cannot change the past, because the past has already been written. But today we can rejoice in bringing her home. This is a day of rejoicing, a day of happiness, a day marking that what

was once lost has now been found. The doors that were not open

to bring Rose home in her lifetime have now been opened wide so

that we could bring her home to rest forever with her family. And

as much as we are celebrating here today, there is another

celebration going on, one in Heaven. I can only imagine how

wonderful that celebration must be. I can see Rose, her mother

and father, her grandparents, her uncles and her brother, my

father with all the rest of her family rejoicing, for their Rose is

Home!!! The angels in Heaven are singing just a little louder

today.

Today also marks the day that I can finally answer a

question I was asked years ago when I was very young. My

grandmother Helen, Rose's mother, who had her own illnesses to

deal with, asked me, "Annie, do you know where Rose Ann is? Do

you think she's all right?" I didn't have the answer for her then, I

didn't know. Well today, today I do know. Today I can say, in

answer to that long-ago question that has always haunted me,

"Yes, grandma, I do know where Rose Ann is and I know that she is all right, because she is home."

Even though I never got to meet Aunt Rose here on earth, I feel that she has walked with me through this journey of bringing her home. Her spirit has guided me every step of the way. She opened each door that we walked through together. Whenever I thought this day wouldn't be possible, there would be another sign, and another door would open, and we would just walk through. Thank you, Aunt Rose, for leading the way.

So on this most joyous of days, we finally get to say the words that Rose waited to hear all her life. Welcome home, Aunt Rose, your family has been waiting for you. Welcome Home.

Rose's headstone in Immanuel Lutheran Cemetery in Mt. Olive, Illinois.

The funeral was a way of giving Rose something. She had never had a special birthday party or a bridal shower, no wedding or baby shower to plan. We had to fit a lifetime of special days into just one occasion. I can only hope it was enough. Her headstone reads, "Rose Ann Pianfetti, Beloved Daughter, Sister and Aunt. Home at last." For truly, after years of enduring and surviving, my aunt is home at last.

Chapter 6

Rose's Story

I had thought that finding and bringing Rose home would be all that Rose would want, but it turned out not to be the case. Rose wanted more than that from me. She needed me to know her story, how her journey had come to be. Her life, sad though it was, was just that, her life. And no one had ever listened to her, had ever given her a chance to tell her story. I began to wonder how I would ever find out what had happened to Rose. Why had her life turned out as it had? Almost all of the people who might have any answers for me were already deceased.

I thought I might find out what I wanted to know when I spoke with one of Rose's state-appointed guardians. But he could tell me very little. If I wanted more information, he told me, I would have to request Rose's records from the State of Illinois. Because her records were mental health records, I would need a court order to obtain them. This would mean getting a judge to issue the court order. For this, I would need an attorney. This all felt very overwhelming and scary, and I could go through this whole process just to find out that there were hardly any records left. Rose was committed in 1953, so it was very possible that no records even existed anymore after all these decades. But it didn't matter. I had made up my mind that no matter what it took, I would find a way to obtain her records.

Where to begin? I decided that calling the county courthouse might be a place to start. As I have stated before, I have been blessed with the guidance of many angels along this journey, and I was about to meet another one. When I called the county courthouse, I was directed to the circuit court clerk. When I told him my aunt's story and why I wanted her records, he was very sympathetic. He asked me to fax over the information I had so far.

After reading what I had sent, he called me back and offered to help in any way he could. I explained that I knew I needed a judge to sign the court order, and I thought he could point me in the right direction. I was extremely hopeful when he said he would show a judge my documents. This was more than I could have asked for, or even dreamed of. This would speed everything up, and I would be able to obtain the records much faster. I was not disappointed. A judge did sign the court order. This was the best news that I could possibly get. With a judge's signature on a court order, no state agency would be able to deny me Rose's records. With this hurdle overcome, my greatest prayer was that her records still existed. I could only hope and pray that there would be enough words in the records to tell me something of what had happened to Rose.

Once I sent the court order requesting the records to the state agency, it was a waiting game. I had hoped it wouldn't take long, but I understood that Rose was admitted long before computers were around. I also understood that there might be

147

no records at all left to read. My waiting paid off when I finally received the packet in the mail. I was extremely optimistic. It was thick, indicating that perhaps there were many pages of records, which is what I was hoping for. I set it down on the table and just stared at it. It felt incredible to finally be looking at what could possibly hold the answers to my many questions. Or it could hold no answers at all. The moment of truth had arrived.

To open the packet and see the stack of typed pages, one after the other, was both exciting and terrifying. As I began to read them, I realized that these were actual interviews conducted not only with Rose, but with members of my family. This was the treasure I had prayed I would find. These pages looked as if they had been typed yesterday, when in fact they had been typed in 1953. That these documents had stood the test of time, been located, then found their way to me is nothing short of a miracle.

Thank you, Aunt Rose, for making sure that I would receive this gift. You entrusted me with your story, even though at times it broke my heart to read it. It was with these typed words that I was able to tell your story. Through her own words and the words of my family of ghosts, I was able to piece together how Rose's story came to be hers. Rose wanted her story to be told. Hers could be the story of other young people her age who were victims of the times they were born in. Her strength and character have been an inspiration to me, this incredibly strong woman who lived through things I can't even imagine and kept carrying on, no matter what. Through bleak, dark, and horrifying times, she continued along, knowing that one day, somehow, she would find her way back home.

After reading Rose's records, I realized that I would also need my grandmother's medical records. Her story was intertwined with Rose's, and I owed both of them a chance to let their story be known. The county clerk again proved invaluable. When I asked if he could also assist me in obtaining my grandmother's records, he didn't hesitate. He got a judge to sign the court order. This was such a blessing as reading both of their records answered many questions for me that wouldn't have been answered if I had only Rose's set of records. The records themselves were the only reason Rose's story could be told. I would've had no way to know what happened all those years ago without the gift of those preserved records.

I have read and re-read both sets of records many times. I am so grateful that they still existed so I could read the exact words that were spoken by my family so many decades ago. The records guided my telling of Rose's story. I know it was no coincidence that they were so well preserved. Rose made sure that I received what I needed, and I am forever grateful to her for that. I can only hope that I have done her justice with these words.

It has been difficult at times to write this story, knowing how deeply my aunt suffered. She survived such darkness and sadness that many in her shoes wouldn't have been able to endure. I have had some people say to me that Rose's life was a waste, that she was so young and had her years stolen from her. Although I understand why people would say that, I don't agree with it. Not at all. Her life, though sad, was full of determination, perseverance, and triumph over sorrows, too many to count. What happened to Rose and to my grandmother happened to many women like them in their era. They were victims of a time and of a generation that did not treat them well or know how to help them.

I like to think that if Rose had been born in this generation, her life would have been much different. With the medical advances we have made, her breech birth most likely would not have caused her the physical disabilities that plagued her all her life. Hopefully, she would've received an accurate diagnosis and the help she so desperately needed.

I've said before that many angels helped me along this journey, and I will forever be grateful to each one of them. Rose is home now, and she made sure I was able to learn what I needed to in order to tell her story. Learning about Rose's life also helped me understand how difficult my father's childhood was and the cause of much of his pain.

I feel I came to know Rose as my aunt, my family, but also as my friend. She has blessed me with her strength, and I feel her spirit with me every day. Because of Rose, I was able to learn so much more about my grandmother and what she endured. My eyes see her differently now. I pray that both these women can rest in peace knowing that no more secrets hold them captive.

And so, as we end this journey, my heart speaks to them both. "Rest well, strong women of my past, safe in the knowledge that your lives were not lived in vain. For in telling your story, we have set our family free."